THRASHER
INSANE TERRAIN

UNIVERSE

THRASHER

Previous Spread: Mr. Incredible, Ty Page goes Double Live Gonzo on the Firestone demo ramp before humpteen thousand heshers at Cal Jam II in the Cali wasteland, 1977.

First published in the United States of America in 2001
by UNIVERSE PUBLISHING
A Division of Rizzoli International Publications, Inc.
300 Park Avenue South
New York, NY 10010

02 03 04 / 10 9 8 7 6 5 4 3

Library of Congress Catalog Number:

Editor: Terence Maikels
Designers: Vincent Arnone and Edward Brogna

Printed in Hong Kong

Insane Terrain is dedicated to Phil Shao, Ruben Orkin and Curtis Hsiang, three skateboarders who gave and got everything they could when called to ride. May they ride on.

INSANE TERRAIN

Terrain is where you find it. Ped X-ing bling bling, Anytown, USA.

"It all started . . ." Lawrence John Hitch III and his skate-board. The perfect vehicle, just when you needed it most.

INTRODUCTION

The stories are always there, it just takes a book to make sure they get written. The reason for the existence of this book is to pass along a part of the story of the skateboard and those who ride them. Anybody who has spent time amongst a dedicated group of skateboarders realizes they have a different way of looking at the world. A different agenda. It's all about the terrain. Skateboarders study and accept the terrain and the architecture that has been placed upon it like no other human beings. Skateboarders are not want for past or future because they are always in the now. "Is it skateable, can we skate it?" Skaters study the curbline from the car as they drive by on the street, drawing a route that hits every inflection, curb cut, crack, and ollie nub along the way. Benches and blocks that go unsat-upon by the few pedestrians rushing by are slid, ground, relished, and appreciated by roving skaters. Steps are to be cleared on the fly and nine will get you ten. You go back to the schoolyard on Saturday mornings to skate the playground banks. There are still enough old schoolers around to make the question "Got any empty pools?" a far better proposition than any drug deal. That skater coming at you down the sidewalk may end up a friend for life.

Skateboarders are certainly not above the classes of nerd, loner, freak, or kook, as everyone is prone to fall into on occasion. But when these varied walks meet in a skate space, look out! Nowhere else will you find a more diverse yet talented group of individuals. Skaters may not have played team sports, joined a gang, or even gone to church. Yet, skaters have infiltrated and influenced art, architecture and music in the same way they would "thrash" a fresh new skate spot. And they know how to fix your car and hook up your stereo.

Insane Terrain is not only a celebration of twenty years of *Thrasher* magazine, but a hail to the spirit and adventure of skateboarding, the spots that are legendary, the skateboarders who have sought them out and the innovators that continue to pusue the basic rush of finding it and sticking it.

Nowhere is the embodiment of the skate spirit found more than in the person of Jake Phelps, *Thrasher* editor for the last ten years. Jake continues to search, seek, and question everything that a skateboard has to offer even as he cracks his body one more time in the pursuit. Generally speaking, Jake has been there and has done it.

If there is a model for this book, other than the pages of *Thrasher*, it would be *National Geographic* magazine. Our intention is to present a clear, awe-inspiring picture into the world of the skaters and the terrain they ride. A collection of photographs that will confound the clueless, wow the masses, and inspire those who would go where no one else has ever been. Flip through this book, look at the pictures, read the captions. This book is not a how-to manual, you'll sort of have to figure that out on your own, and it does not contain any safety precautions, rules, regulations, glossaries of terms, or skatepark lists. Skate safe today, skate again tomorrow, don't stay in one spot too long, and seek and you shall find are about the only advice we will offer in those areas. There are some classic tales and anecdotes to read if you want to go there. Some of the stories, interviews, and editorials from the pages of *Thrasher* magazine have been condensed and edited or updated to fit the context of the times. Photos were chosen to represent a timeless depiction of a skater, at a spot, that connects with all of those who have experienced it or want it.

—Kevin Thatcher, May 2001

Following Spread: "I remember we took my sister's roller skates and mounted them on a two-by-four. . . ." One day, possibly long before this "anything on wheels" derby happened on New York City's East Side in 1952, some kid crashed his skate crate into a tree, and wobbled off down the hill on just a plank with four wheels. The rest is history.

"Find, grind, and leave it behind." Barefootin' rebel pool raider floats through the deep end of a West L.A. bowl in the early 1960s. Although designed for a swim, an empty swimming pool offered the skater "natural" transitions and the freedom of expression afforded by a "magic rolling board." A skater does not trash the terrain that is skated upon, but rather recycles it and makes it live again.

13-1

Facing Page and This Page: While skate-boarders may have borrowed the crude pivot-action truck and axle steering system from roller skate technology, they added a hard surf-styled stance and quickly adapted it to a mode and coda of their own. The sidewalk became the preferred playground and the streets were for free. This suburban Santa Monica, CA, crew posing for a commercial shoot in 1959 had it down, from bun bustin' to band-aids . . . and the chicks dug it.

Previous Spread: When skateboard guru Frank Nasworthy found some urethane skate wheels and took them down to the beach, he found Greg Weaver and the Cadillac Kid and became the poster boy and icon for the spirit of the 1970s surf skater.

Top: Micke Alba returned to the Upland Pipeline one day to relive the glory days and launch out of the pipe on his old Krypstik.

Center: The origins of slash dog style. Tony Altieri works a low-pivotal rotation out of the slot formed by a Southern California reservoir circa 1976.

Bottom: Swedish punk rock skater mixes plaid with his DP stripes for an aggro loading dock drop.

Former famous Playboy Bunny Barbi Benton scoots around the studio lot during production of the ABC-TV series *Sugar*, in which she costarred as Maxx, a rock singer in an aspiring girl group.

Top: Afterschool catamaran comeraderie in San Mateo, CA, 1976.

Center: Mark Conohan barrels into a woodsy ramp somewhere in the Northwest corridor. On big back-yard vert, the backside roll-in was mandatory if you wanted to session with the boys.

Bottom: Underneath the Eiffel Tower in Paris, the duck ponds at Trocadero have welcomed skaters from the world over.

A streetplant session sprouts alongside Mt.
Trashmore in Virginia Beach, VA, 1986.

Curb your dogs. Danny Sargent skated all terrains well but owned the double-sided, red Safeway curb off Market Street in San Francisco, where he worked out often to an appreciative local audience.

Neil Blender was perfectly happy sessioning a parking block all day with a volley of street tricks; some, like this no-comply over an Alhambra Safeway stone, he invented on the spot, named at whim, and took to vert with mind-blowing result.

TWENTY YEARS OF THRASHER MAGAZINE

In November 1980, the crew at High Speed Productions, Inc. printed the first issue of *Thrasher* magazine in San Francisco and started off on a journey into the dense jungle of the magazine publishing world, known for dangerous pitfalls and sinkholes. With enough capital to publish six monthly tabloid-size issues, with or without ad sales, the boys knew it would be a long hard road, with low pay and long hours.

Although the business of skateboarding had dropped off considerably by the end of the 1970s with skateshops and skateparks closing their doors as fast as they had opened them, there was still a healthy, underground contingency of hardcore skaters out there. *Thrasher* didn't orient its coverage toward manufacturers, shopkeepers or parents. Instead, we went for the gut—the kid on the street, the crew skating in your empty swimming pool. That's where skateboarding was in 1980 and we were in on the low end. If there was one skateboarder left out there, then *Thrasher* was for them.

For more than twenty years we've been accepted by this very fickle, very skeptical, very image- and peer-conscious audience that no other magazine has been able to reach on such a large scale. *Thrasher* is theirs. It is by and for them. We incorporate reader writing, art, and photography whenever possible, and our staff consists primarily of young adults who grew up with the mag or acquired their own reputation in the skate world before coming to work here.

Whether it be music, tricks, trends or culture, skateboarders, as a breed, stand fast against a sea of mediocrity. *Thrasher* is, was, and always will be about pushing the edge. This magazine is the longest running, non sell-out Bible of skateboarding simply because it is the unadulterated voice of the streets. In your face, in your backyard, or in the Smithsonian Institute, twenty years of *Thrasher* has changed the world forever.

First issue, *Thrasher Magazine*, January 1981. Skate scene—dead; Cover drawing by KT; printed on rag newsprint; feedback—"black ink rubbed off all over my girlfriends white skirt."

JANUARY 1981

$1.00

THRASHER
SKATEBOARD MAGAZINE ™

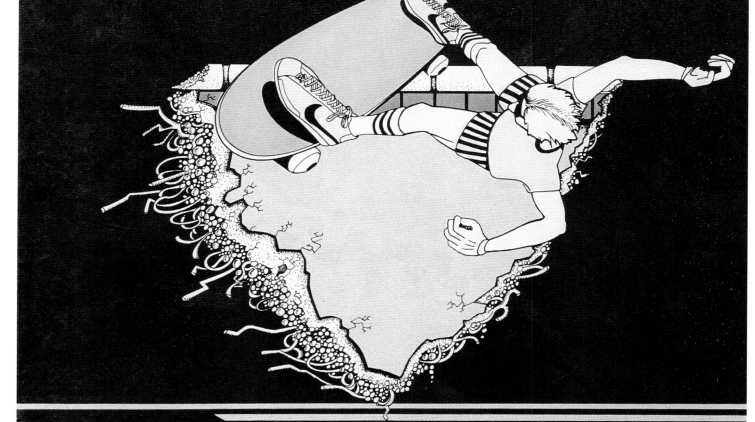

IN THE STREET TODAY

DOWNHILL SKATEBOARD RACING

GOLD CUP FINAL

Northwest skaters take trowel in hand to improve their lot. Abandoned digs in Seattle were patterned after the Burnside Project in Portland.

30

These guys don't skate.

Skaters on patrol pause during Desert Storm, Kuwait.

STAFF

Founding *Thrasher* editor "KT," casual cut back, Uvis Dam, 1976

Michael Henry, Los Altos Pool, 1976

"The Rubberman," Dr. Rick Blackhart, fakie 360 edge-out, Upland Hester Series, 1978

Andy Croft, wailing wall, Daly City, CA, 1975

Original Skate Mechanic, Del 13

Layout master, Mofo, Notre Dame, Paris

The future

Texas ringleader, Jeff "Newtron" Newton, pogo sticking

Kieth Stephenson, aka "Billy Runaway," tucks pipe to pipe

OG city boy and photo pro, Bryce Kanights, burls off his kicker ramp in GG Park, San Francisco

Pierre and skate pup

Thrasher editor Jake Phelps, precarious nollie-oop at Strat's Ramp.

Mr. V brings the bank and a first place check to Caballero at Joe Lope's Backyard Ramp Jam Barbeque and Bake-off, 1984

PHOTOGRAFFITI

PAGE 19   PHOTO A   100%

The Low Road

$400 Million on Wheels

Skateboard World, outside Los Angeles, is a forbidding-looking place, a 3½-acre, concrete moonscape of bone-scorching dunes and valleys, bowls and channels. Day after day, especially during the post-suppermish, it is packed with "carvers" and "boinkers" who pay $2 for

It's a business that's aimed at the very young. The average skateboarder in southern California is only 14, according to one survey, and at Skateboard World, no one over 40 has ever been seen on a board. Yet each of those average skateboarders owns more than $100 worth of

...teboard enthusiasts found a new, arching challenge... terstate 805 in San Diego. The graceful curves of

the huge cement supports for the highway overpass provided a sport for the youngsters to roll on in relative quiet and safety.

Free as a board

Speedracing, slaloming, headstands, pirouettes—that's what skateboarders are into.

Kent Senatore, shallow end involvement at the Ranch.

Getting down to it: At Conservatory Lake in Central Park, a Manhattan skateboard hangout.

Up the wall: *The object is to go as high as you can (this embankment, at a skateboard competition in Asbury Park, N. J., is 15 feet), then turn without falling and zoom down.*

Boarders

Continued from Page 40

But Gregg has recently taken to wearing shoes: "My toe was beginning to feel the pain. My feet just couldn't take it anymore." The boom is now saturated. It's still because California's now mushrooming everywhere else," reports Warren Bolster, editor of SkateBoarder, a Southern California... ...press run of 200,000 ... one last 130 ... including 50 pages of ... and ran to ... to turn away... advertise-ments... now...

...n Sporting Goods ... St. Broadway ... in New York ... Sports just got sales began last ... selling 56 ... ... one curs ... Page 100 skateboards as boards Ed Jimmy ... omers pleasuring... ... time suit up... ... "it's not going in crast splece ... Pargenin's Howard ... author... says ... ... book about skate— ... ... "This time other day ... ... skateboard

...comes off a ramp at a skateboard meet in Uniondale, N. Y. Others ...oards by working up speed, rotating their bodies and jumping.

Doubles: *Like many California skateboarders, these two, doing the "Side Bird," are also surfers.*

Eye contact with Arthur Lake.

Every night fever.   WYNN MILLER

Tony Alva blew minds when he broke the barrel jumping record for the second straight year.

WORLD PROFESSIONAL SKATEBOARD CHAMPIONSHIP

gallery

Tall Tale

Lembert Dome in Tuolomne Meadows is one mountain skateboard enthusiast Dave Liston didn't skate down. But it makes a great story, as told by photographer Fred Clements of Manhattan Beach.

COUNTY ENACTS BAN

State Panel Curbs Motor Skateboard

The same urge that drives youngsters from toy pistol to BB gun to rifle, now has kids on motorized skateboards.

No longer is it simply leg power that propels the slender boards, but a 1.2-horsepower engine that can push them at 20

with human-powered skateboards.

The motorized variety is beginning to proliferate, Oliver said, and Hayden's bill would prevent accidents.

Technically, motorized skateboard operators are subject to

Tues., July 20, 1976

Young skateboard buffs roared down a sidewalk below the Cliff House

---

Skateboard-park developers eye valley's big potential

By GARY SWAN
Staff Writer

Remember the last time a skateboarder almost ran you off the sidewalk with your bag of groceries?

How about the last time you had to jam on your brakes as a skateboarder and its youthful rider came scooting off a driveway?

Haven't you sometimes wished there was a place you could have nicely told them to go?

There soon will be several such places in the San Jose area as enterpreneurs race to beat each other, and perhaps the clock, into the skateboard park field.

In the last year, 40 skateboard parks have sprung up around the country, mainly in Florida and Southern California. In Los Angeles alone, 20 parks are reportedly doing a booming business.

Locally, plans are in varying stages for skateboard parks on Miramonte Avenue near El Camino Real in Mountain View; on South Bascom Avenue in Campbell; and on the south side of Stevens Creek Boulevard between Hwy. 280 and San Tomas Expressway.

State and local governments have begun to come down hard on skateboarders who use the public way. There's a new California law prohibiting use of motorized skateboards on

Existing laws g thority to ban boards from sid er places where of transportation

The county B layed adopting skateboarding only because of felt that such a problem of skat ing faces of da empty reservoir

Kenneth Heg several business $250,000 park (vard, said, "The kids and skateb

Heggem's park parking lot alon of skateboard sp tator areas for w at skateboard tri

The parks will

All skateboard parks must require that participants wear safety gear — helmets, knee pads and elbow pads — to conform to insurance requirements.

Zooming Through an Aqueduct

Where the Skateboards Flow

Phoenix

The giant Central Arizona Project has become something of a headache for some government officials, Indians, farmers and environmentalists, but it's a dream come true to a generation growing up on skateboards.

The $1.7 billion project to carry Colorado river water to central Arizona was cut early this year from the federal budget by President Carter. The project has been restored, however, and work has resumed.

While adults debate whether it really is needed or will supply enough water when system of world."

sheriff's deputies, Bureau of Reclamation and the Ameron Corp, manufacturer of the pipes, skateboard enthusiasts have been sneaking into the pipes near Lake Pleasant every weekend.

"We've put up no-trespassing signs. Deputies are out there checking and citing kids all the time. We have five-to-ten foot barricades at the ends of the pipes, but they still come," said Robert Sevitz, Ameron project manager.

Insurance problems increased, Sevitz said, after an article appeared in Skate Boarder magazine showing the desert discovery with the "pros" doing fakies and kickturns and soaring 11 feet up the big pipes.

Largest in the world, the pipes measure 21 feet in diame-

Skateboarders maneuvered through a section of 'the best skateboard park in the world'

ter inside, are 22 feet long and weigh 225 tons. The ones at the Lake Pleasant site will provide a 5000-foot-long syphon a Agua Fria, New and Salt

"I think the skateboard first discovered the pipes factory near San Clemente, California," Sevitz said. plant manager allowed the try them out and that whetted their appetites."

Although the maxi penalty for trespassing

months in jail and a $300 fine, the lure of the largest pipe in the world to a dedicated skate-

Since then, official permission has been denied moviemakers to use the pipes, he said, but

---

The Skateboard Boom Rolls On

Friends Jaw At Pit Stops

By Michael Grieg

A skateboard-scarred veteran of 15 was comparing wounds and wheels yesterday with other enthusiasts of the big roller revival.

"This is my pride and joy," Burt Witaschek told those who had assembled at Skateboard City, a pit stop shop in the Sunset district that's one of the new phenomena of the booming sport.

He wasn't referring to his $55 Banzai aluminum board with urethane wheels and sealed bearings, capable of whizzing down city hills at 35 miles an hour or more. He

Burt Witaschek, Greg Praeger and Brad Iwafuchi talked shop

By William S.

from his allowance and odd j

Brad Iwafuchi, 15, was d ing some of the best areas i city for skateboarding.

"I like the Cliff House hi out near Hoover Junior High the Junior Museum over street way... I've gotten to spee to 35 miles an hour. Let me tel you do a lot of wobbling at speed."

He and the others said would like to see a skateboard in the city, similar to ones in City and elsewhere.

"It could have a banked c or two to suit those at diff levels of skill," one skateboa said. "Old Playland-at-the-Be now gone, would be a good spo it."

rse, a skateboard

LEE COLE
He said it's here to stay

Jay's radicalization of the Dog Bowl.

THE SKATERS

Everyday unknown, ripper, ruler, trog, and trilobyte.
Slashdog, tech gnar, freshie, and freak. Would-be,
wannabe, will be, and wierdo. Skateboarding brings the
rebels, punkers, outlaws, individualists, and daredevils
together on common ground. When a spot turns up and the
session goes down, you never know who will show up.
Skateboarding brings them out of their holes, but without
skaters . . . we got nothing.

Neil Blender, who routinely made tricks
that nobody has attempted since, creeps
past the edge of Del Mar Skatepark's
fabled hole.

Christian Hosoi, glamour boy of the eighties

Jay Adams and another young ripper from Venice area, George Watanabe, diggin' the scene

Peter Smolik is a modern pro skateboarder having a good time.

Jovontae Turner stylin' chopped Van's and frayed baggies, setting the style for a new street crew to follow.

Above: Bucky Lasek gettin' evil during lean times on the vert circuit.
Right: Brothers of different mothers. Texas pride: Todd Prince, Jeff Phillips, Ken Fillion, and John Gibson—all for one, care for none, just havin' fun.

STYLE

The first time you step on a skateboard pretty much determines whether one is regular foot (left forward) or goofy (right forward). After that it's all a matter of style, interpretation, skill, and balls. And you can bet your buds are going to be critiquing your technique all the way. Push mongo-foot or lead with your fists and take it on the chin. Six gun, lead-foot, cringer, hinger, sasquatch, stinkbug, shit-footer, stomper, natural, styli, or squidly—hey, if you're at least skating—who cares?

Sidewalk surfin' revisited. Scott Oster sets his line and his Air 1's with a high-speed four-wheel drift across the lip of "Charlene's," another secret spot in the hills above skate mecca Los Angeles.

Jake Phelps lays it down at HP Ramp, San Francisco.

Jeff Phillips shows a lot of pop for a big guy and a stylish tuck through a tight square corner.

Nobody looked like Craig Johnson and few will ever skate like him. Break time on the banks at a public skatepark outside Melbourne.

Alan "Ollie" Gelfand may have brought the no-handed air to the front, but he could grab 'em with the best at Surf Expo in Orlando, Florida.

Unsafe at any speed. Simple skate technology has inspired countless widgets and contraptions, none as good as a wood plank pivoting over four urethane wheels.

Gonz's high ollie grab over Lance Mountain's slash grind, during this night-time mini frenzy near Melbourne, OZ, was neither planned nor accidental, as Hosoi will attest.

Mark "Gator" Rogowski had the skills to perform the frontside Rocket Air in Tony Hawk's face at Torquay Ramp Riot, Australia.

Wade Speyer in thrift store attire is the king of pop for a hand-on ollie 180 down city streets.

"You don't hang up, ever," says Mark Gonzales about the roto board he cooked up one afternoon.

There's a fringe element surrounding the skateboard scene that's always good for a laugh and even the occasional sick trick. They may be hangers or lurkers, used-to-skates or everyday nightmares, but just give 'em an elbow to the rib and a few encouraging words and watch them go off.

"There are those who have fallen, and those who will fall." Scotty B looks it right in the eye during an unfortunate dirtboarding accident, Lee Vining, CA, 1993.

FREAK SHOW

Dropping in. Dave Hackett holds the line for a special delivery in NYC, 1987.

the new hot skater

Christian Hosoi and Pat Ngoho getting rave reviews in Japan.

Skaters come and go, especially some who turn pro. After you've waded through all the flash-in-the-pan, one-trick wonders and would-be number ones, the free product, board royalties, and shoe deals—there are a handful of skateboarders whose names are always mentioned as legend. Over the years, there have been those whose skating and manner stand out above the rest. They turn up heat at any session and raise the bar at any contest they choose to enter. Skaters who can win at will and make it or break it on command, leaving jaws dropped and hearts stopped, deserve everything they get out of skating because they've given so much more.

TONY ALVA

MARK GONZALES

In a hot, dirty parking lot at the first Sacto streetstyle contest in 1985, a kid named Mark Gonzales introduced his own brand of skating to the world. Over the next fifteen years he went from being a little scrub to the king of modern-day street skating. Gonz lives in a world that few could ever comprehend. A Sharpie, an old Sims Taperkick, Baby Cujo, a telephone, and a fax machine are all he needs to get by.

MARK GONZALES

JAY ADAMS

The central element—the only one of any importance—is that Adams remains one of the great enigmas in the world of skateboarding. A prime innovator throughout the seventies and much sought after as a commercial entity, Jay seemingly made every effort to avoid the "successful life." During that fat period, when countless less talented sorts made big bucks off skating, Adams meticulously sought only undiluted, uncensored, and uncomplicated thrills. Much to the promoter's chagrin, Jay would regularly choose to disappear off into the tropics rather than keep in line for the movie gigs, mag covers, and assorted other trappings of fame and fortune.
—Lowboy, August 1982

JAY ADAMS

TONY HAWK

TONY HAWK

If one person has dominated the sport, it's Tony Hawk. Spit upon by Duane as a child, even as he performed Miller Flips at the scumline of Whittier Skatepark's keyhole pool, Hawk came to manhood by redefining the art of vertical skateboarding. His unbelievable legacy of trick development includes: ollie 540s, 720s, kickflip 540s, and the 900. Hawk will live forever as the supreme technician and as an ambassador of modern skateboarding's acceptance of it during its prime time.

CHRISTIAN RASHA HOSOI
Legend in skateboard circles, Christian Hosoi's status has busted far beyond the boundaries of just those in the know. The poster boy for skate style throughout the eighties; consistent top three contender at every major vert, street, or mini-ramp contest; the Hosoi air show was consistently over eight feet—back to back as he traveled the world spreading a positive vibe about skateboarding. After every event, contest, or demo—long after everyone was already out—Christian was there, signing autographs, talking to skaters; Christ was always respectful to moms, dads, and fans alike. Christian Hosoi could skate any terrain and charged every skate situation with a precision and flair that said "superstar" and backed it up with the baddest skating you'd ever seen. In the history of the sport, no name is more synonymous with power, style, and finesse than Holmes.

CHRISTIAN HOSOI

STEVE CABALLERO

Caballero showed up at Campbell Skatepark sheathed in plastic and padding from fingertip to toe cap and proceeded to light a fire that burns to this day. Highlights include: frontsides across the gorge-like Winchester Pool channel, Caballerials, and more signature moves than any other skater. Caballero won professional skateboard contests in the 1970s, 1980s, and 1990s, and is now pacing himself into his fourth decade of skateboarding. He is a certified Bones Brigadeer general, musician, producer, husband, and daddy, not in any particular order, though hundreds of thousands of his fans know him simply as one of skateboarding's all-time bests.

STEVE CABALLERO

DUANE PETERS

Stabbed, beaten, broken, and blood-
ied, Duane Peters has definitely paid
his dues. He's invented more tricks
than he can remember and done
things few will ever forget. To this
day, his style is unapologetically
old school, and you can bet he
doesn't give two O'Henry's what
anyone thinks.

DUANE PETERS

Eric Koston's Number Ones

#1 Trick: Rolling away.
#1 Vegetable: Spinach.
#1 Skater from the Seventies: Eddie Elguera.
#1 Appliance: TV.
#1 Video Part: Mark Gonzales, *Video Days*.
#1 Companion Animal: Dog.
#1 Relative: Mom.
#1 Pool Move: Backside one-footed carve grind.
#1 Excuse: It's too dark.
#1 Religion: Buddhism.
#1 Contest Obstacle: Hotel.

#1 Hiding Place: Home.
#1 Sea Creature: Manatee.
#1 Piece of Furniture: Couch.
#1 Ridiculous Purchase: House.
#1 Meal While in Germany: Chinese food.
#1 Phone Call: Girlfriend.
#1 Reason to Quit: Someone telling you that they made you.
#1 Childhood Hero: Luke Skywalker.
#1 Annoyance: Traffic.
#1 Vacation Spot: Thailand.
#1 Pet Name: Billie.
#1 Plan for the Future: Retire.

ERIC KOSTON

ERIC KOSTON

Eric Koston came to the scene during a period in the late eighties when skateboarding was flat and ripe for a change. Change came in the form of a next generation of super-talented, super-tech board pilots that made skate spots appear where none had existed before and turned tricks that had not been comprehended. Suddenly skaters were turning pro with a video clip and contests were out. So, Koston went out and schooled the best in every contest he entered *and* got it on video.

OMAR HASSAN

OMAR HASSAN
From Blockhead to Black Label, Omar led the early 1990s crossover legions by taking the best of vert and the budding technicality of street straight to the new era of minis. The protégé of Caballero, an all-around nice guy, and a winner of bowl and pool contests even to this day, Omar hasn't laid back after the guard switched over but has organized the change himself.

SEAN SHEFFEY

SEAN SHEFFEY

Skaters today use the term "tech-gnar" to describe someone who has the ability to go big and fast, all while throwing down technical wizardry. When the *Life* video came out in 1992, an eighteen-year-old unknown, who would soon be recognized by the world as "Sheff," burned the screen with huge backside ollies over parking lot islands. If you see him coming at you, get outta the way because big Sheff doesn't care. If there's some fun, he's gonna have it.

BOB BURNQUIST

After winning the first pro contest he ever entered by making everyone care and want to hide their eyes at the same time, blazing Brazilian Bob Burnquist has quickly gone on to mark out a place in skateboard history that his alone. His mastery of all terrains, and his ambidextrous innovation on vert, make it no wonder that Bob is Tony Hawk's favorite skater.

BOB BURNQUIST

C.K.N.

WADE SPEYER

GEOFF ROWLEY

GEOFF ROWLEY
Geoff Rowley is everything I think a pro skater should be. He's a good friend and one of my favorite people to skate with. He's always pushing himself to the limit.
—Chad Muska

WADE SPEYER
One of the first times I ever skated with Wade outside a demo/contest atmosphere was when he first started riding for Powell. Steve Sherman and I drove up to his house to shoot video and went to some of his spots with him. I remember one edge that was on the side of a LONG driveway. It was one of those wide edges that your trucks barely clear when you slide it (it was too rough to grind). You needed a pretty high ollie up to it, then a steady slide to the end—actually you had to come off before the end or you'd wind up in the plants. The middle part was probably six to eight feet off the ground. I tried it a couple of times but I couldn't make it through the middle without ketching out. You just never knew if your board was gonna stop and send you head first off the side. Wade made it first try: clean all the way through—only he had to do it frontside.
—Tony Hawk

BOMBIN' HILLS

Layed out. Lee Danzie casually no-looks while careening down a mountain on what looks like an auto shop creeper you might use to slide under your car, but not at sixty miles an hour.

Tony Alva leads with his chin, dropping into a Beverly Hills bowl at top speed. Whatever the situation, whatever the terrain, Alva is game for skating and he will make his presence known.

Mainlining. Fred Smith speed carves a roadside Roxbury ditch in Boston, MA.

SIDEWALK SURFIN'

An abandoned, bleached white motel pool on the shores of the Salton Sea is close to Heaven-on-earth for some skaters—mere mortals want nothing to do with it.

One of the most popular skate locales has been the drained swimming pool. Long after the kiddies with their life preservers and the yuppies with their poolside parties have deserted their pools, some of these structures, now drained, have excellent curves and gradations and quickly become the perfect hangouts for skaters.

Jeff Phillips went on to become one of the world's best vert champions but his roots were skating Texas plaster with the crew.

A unique backyard pool configuration in a swank golf-course community outside Honolulu does not go unnoticed, or unskated, by the local boys.

Still guilty during more innocent times. Empty pools were abundant on the West Coast during drought years in the seventies. Andy Croft test carves Los Altos pool before kooks ripped out the coping, sawed off the ladders, painted it orange, and got photos in the mag.

One of the great pool skaters,
Ruben Orkin, grinds a perfect
kidney keeper.

Outtake from June 1984 cover shoot. Mark "Gator" Rogowski hit this freshly drained, kinked-out backyard pool from every angle including this lapover into the shallows.

Attack with enough speed and snap, and something's got to give. David Hackett power ollies make-or-break style over the "death box."

Ruben Orkin performs the delicate alleyoop Rube-a-dupe, grinding backwards into the shallow end.

Shallow end frontside grind, over the steps . . . doesn't get any tougher, but seasoned pool player Royce Nelson makes it look smooth.

Mark Jones takes a smooth line through the heel of an abandoned L-pool in the desert that is Southern California.

Christian Hosoi lays back hard on some cruel square coping during a morning shade pool hit in Phoenix.

Julien Stranger stands up to the bur
that is C-pool in Cambridge,
Massachusetts. Note the twelve-foo
mark, kinked tranny, and Julien's lin
that started before the death star
and carried him over the box.

Border patrol. If you can't locate this pool on the Mexi-Cali border after seeing the clues in this photo, then you don't skate . . . or don't care. It's probably been filled with dirt anyway, and the building in the background is the local police department. Just don't tell them we sent you.

Buena Vista pool near Santa Cruz has been skated off and on for more than thirty-five years. Al Losi skated Buena one day.

Feeling no pain. Barefoot, baked, and mud-caked in the Hawaiian sun, Kale Sandridge works any empty pool that crosses his path. Kale rips bowls so thoroughly sometimes even he doesn't know which direction his stance is going.

Government issue. Brian Brannon applies a hands-on approach to the unique beveled transition and spit gutter configuration of Bastrop pool at an abandoned army outpost in Texas.

The abundant square footage of
the receiving pool at San Jose's
Raging Waters slide park is
scoured for a rare throw down.

Mike McGill and Tony Hawk perform side by side 540s on a shaky demo ramp before thousands of fans in downtown Sydney, Australia.

To have your own skatespot right in the backyard is an attainable dream that many saavy skaters have realized. Pop out of bed, put on the coffee, feed the cats, and strap on the pads and helmet. You built it, you skate it, you rule it. No other backyard "sport" has caused such a proliferation of crafted structures on such a scale as skateboarding. From building driveway quarter pipes to mega Chin-styled, multi-bowled, and spined monoliths, skateboarders continue to demonstrate the positive effects of mixing creativity with a little insanity.

Kasai High. Lester would go bio until he exploded but his third air was usually clocking in the ten-foot range like this one over the blue monster at Houston Skatepark.

Christian Hosoi, tipped out frontside Indy bone, on his ramp. Los Angeles, CA

Wade's garage, Concord, CA, 1994

Previous Spread: Sunday picnic. A three-day demo on the Shake billboard half pipe inside the Formula 1 circuit in Adelaide, Australia, was a rather casual affair. Lee Ralph and Mark Gonzales are i
there somewhere.

re you ready for some football? Well, no. Little fans dragged along to daddy's games remember the halfpipe on Monday night and the names of the inverted demo dogs who performed. Fifteen
ars later, ratings down—skateboarding up. Thanks ABC—you did rule.

One of the world's best in any skateboarding arena, Phil Shao said that this ollie to top bar out of the "killer capsule" in Madrid, Spain, was the gnarliest thing he had done in a long time.

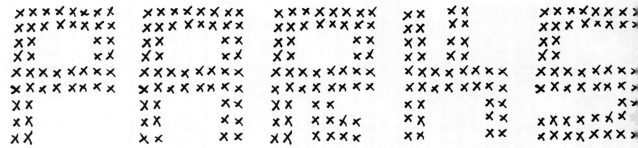

Good, Bad . . . Ugly. Except for Kona Skatepark in Jacksonville, Florida, none of more than two hundred commercial skateparks built in the United states in the late seventies survived the bulldozer. Does the same fate await the hundreds of public skate facilities being installed across the land today? Some are so poorly designed as to be dangerous.

Aproador bowls in Rio de Janiero straddle the peninsula between world-class beach real estate.

Weston Creek on the Australian skatepark trail
offers up a myriad of finally radiused and crisp-
ipped possibilities for Dan Drehobl to float over.

Young Tommy Guerrero knuckle drags an early grab over the hip of a sweet snake run at Victoria in Milpitas, CA.

Worldly perfect. Skateparks can be fun when they are prepared and served well done, no frills, by a competent staff. Livingston, Scotland boasts one of the first and foremost government-sponsored dishes and Livi's designs still hold Alan Petersen's air eighteen years after Caballero and the Bones Brigade cut the ribbon.

Fly by. Bob Burnquist ollie crosses the gap at Guara Country Club, on the road to Rio from São Paulo, Brazil.

Lee Ralph is a big man to be
grinding the tight and deadly
1/4 pipe at Nunawading, outside Melbourne.

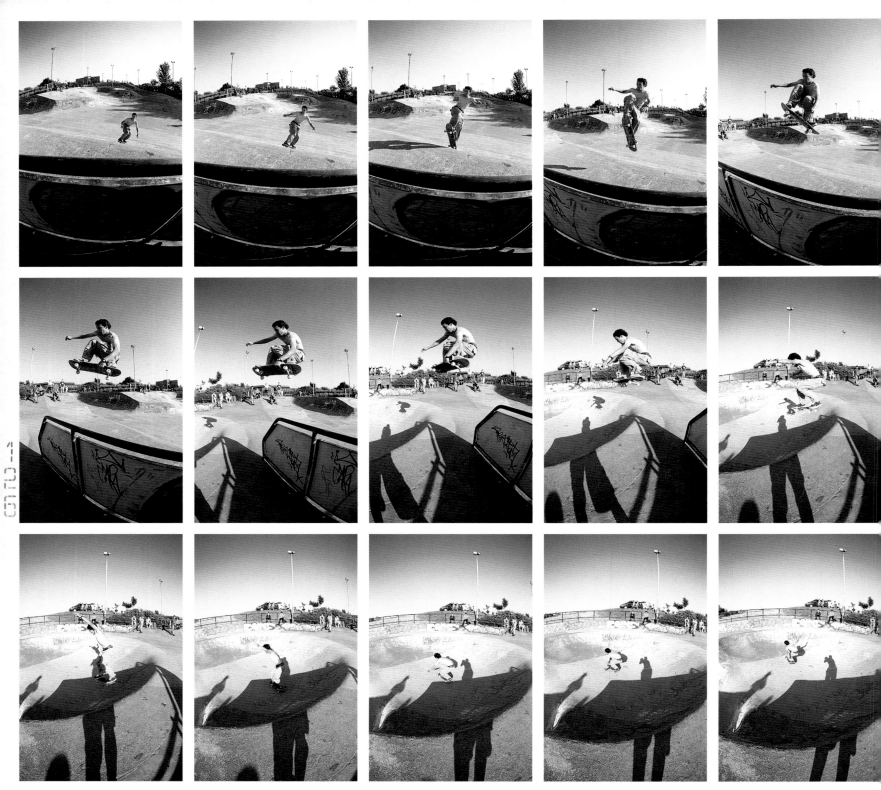

Another level. Phil Shao hit a zone that few have ever reached with this ollie to frontside grab over everything at another well-received public skatepark.

Judah Oaks, public park flight over one of the many in Vancouver BC, Canada. Small towns can get things done quicker and skateparks are popping up at an alarming rate. The average wait for a bad park in the big city: eight to ten years from first request to opening-day air raid.

This Page and Facing Page: Mark Scott launches out and over a public park he designed and constructed in Lincoln City, Oregon. Some claim its crisp and fast contours to be the gnarliest yet.

Now living outside San Diego, world champ Bob Burnquist often returns to his homeland spots in South America to rework a line like this down time tail drop inbetween traffic jams.

STREETS

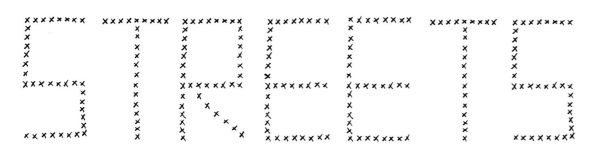

A curb is an obstacle until you grind across it. A wall is but a ledge until you drop off it. A cement bank is a useless slab of concrete until you shred it. A street is another downhill to be tucked. A multi-level garage is built for cars until a gang of skaters discovers it. You've got to give the streets fair due—rolling is way cooler than walking. Don't restrict your boundaries—skate architecture is everywhere—grind every edge. You've gotta find all the lines you can.

Cairo Foster may have moved the dumpster into his path down the sidewalk . . . skaters have been known to exhibit such behavior.

ll aboard. Matt Hensley had just graduated from the academy when he found this roller coaster rail in Mission Beach near San Diego, before e became a real bona-fide pro street star.

Flashpoint. Jamie Thomas usually catches up to any reputation that preceeds him but stays pretty humble about routinely launching himself down thirty-five feet of landscaping for a living.

Most pros can stick the tre-flip on ugly inclines such as this one, but Rick Howard managed to reproduce his *Thrasher* cover outtake with a little yellow plastic banana board.

Hubba MC. Coming up together in San Francisco, Mike Carroll got to know Hubba Hideout's famous ledges pretty well, so this switch backside for Smith wasn't too much of a problem. The Hubba ledge has gone on to become a featured element of every new skatepark and contest design.

New school. When the street scene came to the front in the early nineties Jesse Martinez escaped from Venice and unleashed a furious assault on every plane. Here, "the Mess" shows several hundred locals at a schoolyard demo in Honolulu how to hit the bricks and make a wall walk heli-spin work for you.

What is that railing for anyways? Danny Fuenzalita sees no other way around another useless barrier on the sidewalk of life.

Street titan. Unmatched in his crisp innovative boardwork and creativity, Rodney Mullen only needs a few square feet of EMB stage to rip, but his skating has influenced the scene for miles.

San Francisco skaters eventually troweled ready mix concrete to form a transitioned bowl among a ring of barricades on the city waterfront. Marcus crooked grinds either way.

Knock knock? It's Josh Kalis, passing overhead and over rail from off a downhill snap.

Spot check. "New Spots" do come up everyday when you ride a skateboard. Ibon Marino cleans a rugged gap in textbook fashion at the latest gift from the city of San Francisco.

Mark Gonzales does the tailfin slide, in the rain, that was heard 'round the world from Willamette, Oregon.

A little goes a long way. Quim Cardona ollies the small bump at Fort Miley in San Francisco's Presidio and makes it stale and shifted.

All terrain. Bridging the gap between street and vertical skating Noah Peacock sticks to a city wall and eyes his line for the pedestrian sidewalk slalom and the ensuing high speed hill bomb beyond. Just another typical run down to the corner store in "the biggest skatepark in the world"—San Francisco.

Paid in full. John Cardiel owes nothing in dues and doesn't think about his bank account when trying to conquer new challenges like a kinked rail on Pot Hill in San Francisco. **Results:** Cards: one ad photo, no cover, possible concussion.

Get there before it's gone. *Thrasher* receptionist Jen Franks spied this spot from the bus to work one morning. Crews were dispatched, mounted on soft red "Krypto" wheels to traverse the flesh-eating finish of what turned out to be an earthquake-proof skyscraper foundation excavation. Who would have known about this site, except skaters like Toad (**left**) and Justin Strubing on night watch.

Natas Kaupas banks to grind while on patrol through the back lots and alleys of West L.A.

Fully tubed. Jesse Martinez watches Kelly Jackson work a section amongst a grove of full pipes in Westchester, CA.

Fence jumpin' time. The U.S. Army Corps of Engineers has no competition when it comes to building skate terrain, and they like to keep their secrets. Only skateboarders would brave to obtain the maps and test the waters.

U.S. PROPERTY
NO
TRESPASSING

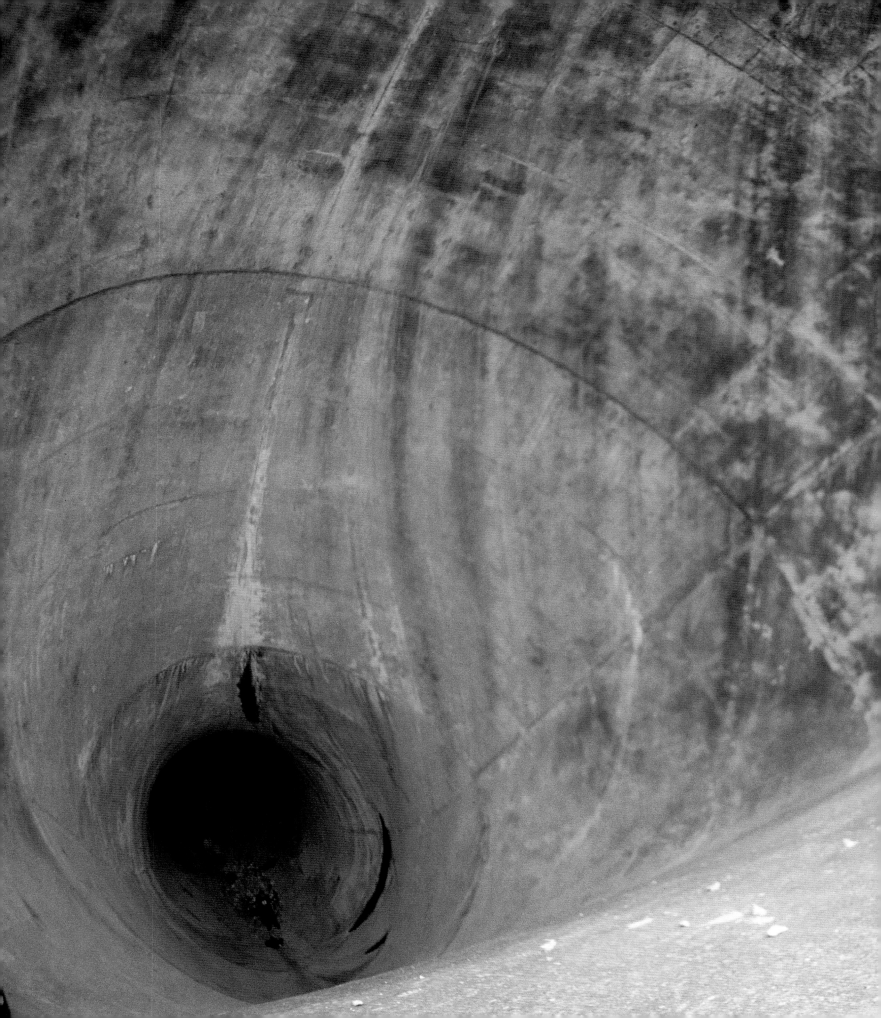

What a way to go. Someday, someone will take the ultimate drop-in at Pipa' Grande in Central Cali. The few skaters who have even ventured to perch themselves at the spillway lip inevitably end up debating which line to take—straight it or corkscrew the roof.

Journey to the center of the Earth. Eric Joy digs deep to find the smoothest walls inside Pipa Grande.

Because it's there. Another expedition to the Mother of all, Glory Hole.

King of the Badlands and the Great Lord of pool and pipeology, Steve Alba still plays the flat walls at the mouth of Baldy Pipeline like no other and crosses "the line" beyond where even grafitti can't reach. Salba now makes his home in Ontario, California, gateway to the "Inland Empire" (a developer's term for paved desert), just down the Arrow highway from the ruins of the Upland Pipeline Skatepark and at the center of a fifty-mile circle of sprawl that encompasses more prime pool, pipe, park, drainage, and street terrain than the rest of the earth combined.

Glory be. Folklore has it that only two people have died at Glory Hole and neither were skaters. One woman got sucked down in a little rowboat and another person tumbled down the rock face and was slammed to death at the mouth.

Craig Johnson testing and in-
specting the flat wall outside the
mouth of the Ammo pipe.

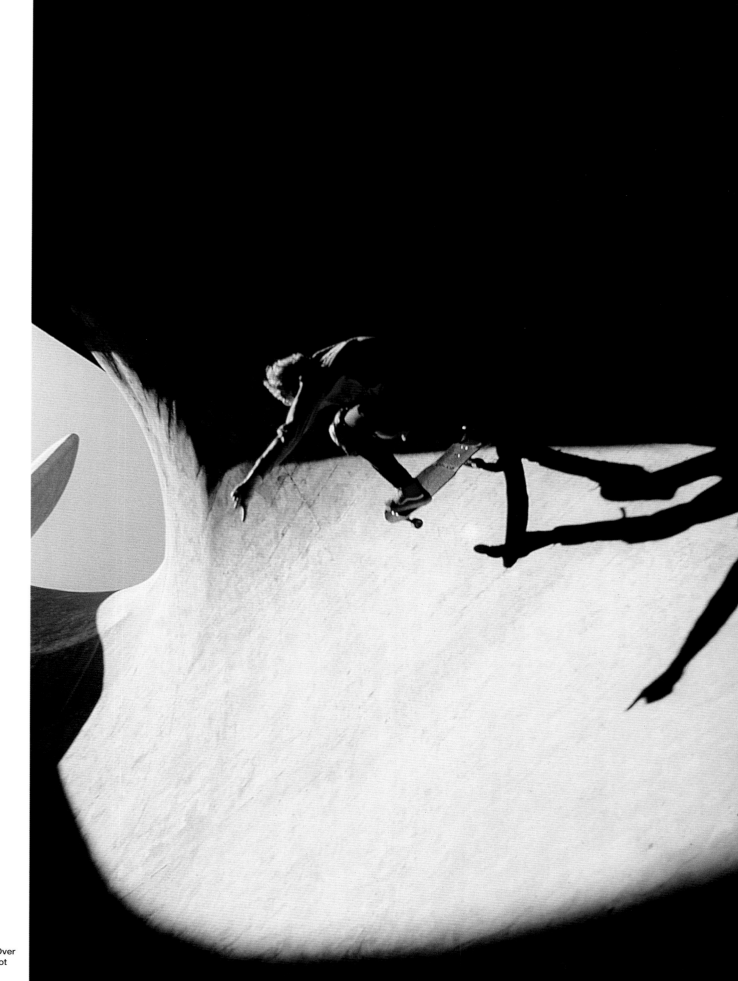

Messin' with Texas. Typifying the Lone Star big and tall skate-style John "Tex" Gibson attacks the upper quadrants of the Ammo Pipe's cathedral-like elbow with respectful and unhurried grace. Over amp here and it's a seventeen-foot space walk back down to earth.

All terrain champion John Cardiel is beyond the point of no return and still climbing past vertical. Once you start clocking in towards 10:30 the cost of trying to make it is cheaper than the damages if you bail.

Reigning it in. George Orton took many full body slams while launching his patented frontside airs out of the wrong side of Upland's pipe. Pipeline's deep terrain served as proving ground for vert jocks for more than fifteen years but served up many skaters with career-ending body damage.

Land of the Giants. A behemoth cylinder "somewhere in the Southwestern desert." If the skater standing at the mouth is just under six feet tall then the massive maw of the giant Texas tube might be pushing thirty-five feet. This is one of two photos of the only known session there in 1978.

Going underground. Alan Petersen
ollie falls from the roof at Glory Hole.

TERRAIN OF THE INSANE

Man, during his productive stages, tends to redecorate the world with curious structures. By taking a transient, sometimes irrational, or utopian idea and turning it into a concrete perm, he leaves his mark on the world. Sometimes these ideas pay off, leaving an accomplishment of dubious achievement—form following function. Other times, these finished products serve their purpose but lie in state for many years, sometimes decades, between uses. Of course many fresh ideas just grow old, leading to abandonment, yet the cost of deconstruction in modern dollars can be as high as that which built it yesteryear. It is many of these structures that the skaters of the world seek out and call their own. Discovery of a forgotten spot leads the skateboarder to hours of the good life. For it is they who are capable of seeing the real beauty in the slopes and surfaces of these concrete creations. And when it comes to riding such "natural terrain," each session provides insight into the irony of what constitutes perfectly skateable terrain. For, as always, those places not intended for skateboarding always seem better than the terrain specifically conceived for the board (*i.e.,* skateboard parks).

A secret skate spot never stays that way for very long and many of the large and legendary skate places are not all that secret to begin with. It may be right in front of your face, or under your feet. You may have even touched it already. Other times, a well known (and watched) swimming pool, spillway or twenty-stair block suddenly becomes available. One thing you can always bet on is that skaters will maximize any opportunity that comes their way. Yet while the attitude is Skate & Destroy, the credo is "Take nothing but pictures (or video), leave only grinds." Or, "one good session deserves another."

Following Spread: Terrain is where you find it. Skaters definitely look at the world from a different perspective, as this overview of a casual Sunday session in a Newport, Rhode Island, boatyard will attest. It seems the woodhull molds for a certain model of fiberglass racing sloop were deemed to be skateworthy on close inspection.

Conquered. John Cardiel's expression tells the story as he's all over this long nose slide on a steep California street stair ledge that few had even thought of attempting.

Previous Spread: The Seattle Hat is a novelty spot that has been busted on and off for years. Does anybody know if it survived the earthquake of 2001?

Pool with pop. Eric Nash's ollie to tail grab out of the Jelly Bean Bowl proves that a small corner of any yard could host some dynamic skate terrain.

Dinosaur Country. Get-A-Way Skatepark in Huntsville, AL, was another seventies skatepark that barely saw its day before it was demolished.

Sliding the fall-line of an endless New Mexico ditch, 1990.

Above: Peter Hewitt taps out of the pipe end where the fun really begins.

Right: Club Med for the ride crew. Viva Quito, Ecuador, for designing a sick skatepark that doubles as a flood channel and is a sure lure for those nomads who would go to the ends of the earth to wheel its curves.

Following Spread:
Left: Loop of death. End of the day, several skaters had already been carried out on stretchers when Bob Burnquist charged the made for TV attraction in Tampa, FL, switchstance, nailed it, and sent everyone home.

Right: Overview of a one-use contest contraption dubbed the "bow," used for the NSA traveling road show contest series in the late eighties.